GIFTED & TALENTED®

*To develop
your child's gifts
and talents*

PUZZLES & GAMES

FOR CRITICAL AND CREATIVE THINKING

A Workbook for Ages 4-6

Written by June Bailey

Illustrated by Paul Manchester

Lowell House
Juvenile
Los Angeles
CONTEMPORARY
BOOKS
Chicago

Manufactured in the United States of America

ISBN 1-56565-129-4

10 9 8 7 6 5 4 3 2

GIFTED & TALENTED® WORKBOOKS will help develop your child's natural talents and gifts by providing activities to enhance critical and creative thinking skills. These skills of logic and reasoning teach children **how** to think. They are precisely the skills emphasized by teachers of gifted and talented children.

Thinking skills are the skills needed to be able to learn anything at any time. Unlike events, words, and teaching methods, thinking skills never change. If a child has a grasp of how to think, school success and even success in life will become more assured. In addition, the child will become self-confident as he or she approaches new tasks with the ability to think them through and discover solutions.

GIFTED & TALENTED® WORKBOOKS present these skills in a unique way, combining the basic subject areas of reading, language arts, and math with thinking skills. The top of each page is labeled to indicate the specific thinking skill developed. Here are some of the skills you will find:

- Deduction — the ability to reach a logical conclusion by interpreting clues

- Understanding Relationships — the ability to recognize how objects, shapes, and words are similar or dissimilar; to classify and categorize

- Sequencing — the ability to organize events, numbers; to recognize patterns

- Inference — the ability to reach logical conclusions from given or assumed evidence

- Creative Thinking — the ability to generate unique ideas; to compare and contrast the same elements in different situations; to present imaginative solutions to problems.

How to Use GIFTED & TALENTED® WORKBOOKS

Each book contains activities that challenge children. The activities vary in range from easier to more difficult. You may need to work with your child on many of the pages, especially with the child who is a non-reader. However, even a non-reader can master thinking skills, and the sooner your child learns how to think, the better. Read the directions to your child and, if necessary, explain them. Let your child choose to do the activities that interest him or her. When interest wanes, stop. A page or two at a time may be enough, as the child should have fun while learning.

It is important to remember that these activities are designed to teach your child **how to think**, not how to find the right answer. Teachers of gifted children are never surprised when a child discovers a new "right" answer. For example, a child may be asked to choose the object that doesn't belong in this group: a table, a chair, a book, a desk. The best answer is **book**, since all the others are furniture. But a child could respond that all of them belong because they all could be found in an office or a library. The best way to react to this type of response is to praise the child and gently point out that there is another answer, too. While creativity should be encouraged, your child must look for the best and most **suitable** answer.

GIFTED & TALENTED® WORKBOOKS have been developed and written by teachers. Educationally sound and endorsed by leaders in the gifted field, this series will benefit any child who demonstrates curiosity, imagination, a sense of fun and wonder about the world, and a desire to learn. These books will open your child's mind to new experiences and help fulfill his or her true potential.

Look at the pictures. Find the word that matches each picture in the box below. Try to write the correct word on the line next to each picture.

cat	mouse	deer	fox	cow	bunny
frog	bug	cheese	dog	skunk	baby	tree
bike	wagon	egg	toy	girl

Now draw two of your own pictures. Write the matching words on the lines. You can do some more on another piece of paper.

_____   _____

Look closely at the Thinker Blinker puzzle.

Color the parts that rhyme with **ad** red.

Color the parts that rhyme with **ed** blue.

Color the parts that rhyme with **am** yellow.

Color the parts that rhyme with **at** green.

THINKER BLINKER

Read each clue. Then find a rhyming word that matches the clue in the word box below. Try to write that word on the line next to the clue. Can you find any other rhyming words?

Think of a word that rhymes with **tag**.
It can be red, white, and blue.   _____

Think of a word that rhymes with **wish**.
It lives in the water.   _____

Think of a word that rhymes with **silk**.
You can drink it.   _____

Think of a word that rhymes with **meat**.
You walk on two of them.   _____

Think of a word that rhymes with **blows**.
You have ten, and they can wiggle.   _____

Think of a word that rhymes with **dog**.
It is green and lives near a pond.   _____

Think of a word that rhymes with **man**.
You can cook eggs in it.   _____

mat	frog	girl	pan
fish	log	boy	feet
milk	toes	flag	can
bag	hat	fog	nose
seat	van	sag	sat

Read the sentences below. They are missing words. Now look at the word box. Which rhyming words will you choose? Try to write the words on the lines.

Little Boy Blue, come blow your _____ , the sheep's in the meadow, the cow's in the _____ .

The kitten was _____ in the tall corn. Sally gave the kitten her _____ , _____ blanket.

torn	corn	horn
	worn	born

Circle the picture that starts with the sound of **bl**.

Circle the picture that starts with the sound of **cl**.

Circle the picture that starts with the sound of **dr**.

  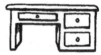

Circle the picture that starts with the sound of **tr**.

  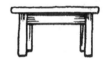

Circle the picture that starts with the sound of **sp**.

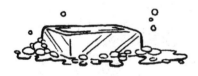 

Circle the picture that starts with the sound of **gl**.

For some sounds, did you circle 2 pictures? Good for you!

Color this spring picture. Circle what does not belong. How can you tell?

Color this summer picture. Circle what does not belong.
How can you tell?

Color this fall picture. Circle what does not belong. How can you tell?

Color this winter picture. Circle what does not belong. How can you tell?

Look at the animals on this page and the next. Which animals belong on a farm? Which animals belong in a forest? Which animals belong at the circus? You decide.

Write the correct number on each animal. Write **1** for farm, **2** for forest, and **3** for circus.

There are 10 children in Allison's class. For Valentine's Day, Allison's mom bought a box of cards for her to send. There were 10 cards in the box.

Allison sent 1 valentine to each child in the class. There is 1 valentine left in the box. Why? Who didn't get a card?

Timmy is having a birthday party. His family is making paper chains to decorate the house. Look at Timmy's mom and dad, his big brother, Jim, his big sister, Sue, and his little brother, Andy.

Whose chain is the longest? _____

Whose chain is the shortest? _____

How many chains are there? _____

How many circles are there in Jim's chain? _____

How many circles are there in Andy's chain? _____

Color the paper chains. Make Jim's chain the same color as Andy's. Make Timmy's the same color as Dad's. Make Mom's and Sue's chains rainbow colors.

Look at the long line of boots. Use the clues to color them all in.

3 pairs of boots are red.
2 pairs of boots are green.
4 pairs of boots are purple.
1 pair of boots is yellow.
2 pairs of boots are orange.

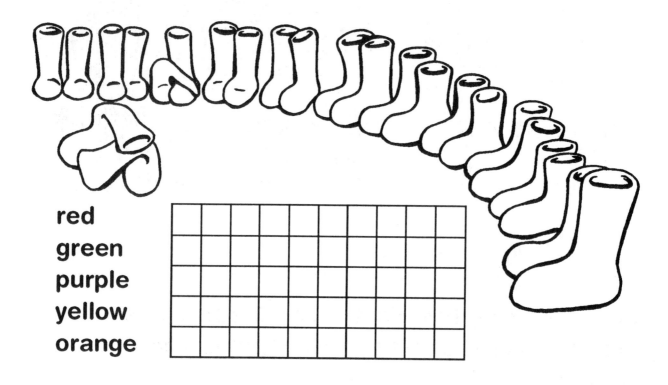

red
green
purple
yellow
orange

Now color in the bar graph. Use the clues to color 1 square for **each** boot in every color. Think carefully!

Which bar is the longest? How many colored squares does it have? _____

Read the clues below. Write each child's name under the correct picture. Color the balloons by following the clues.

_____ _____ _____ _____ _____

Bennie has curly hair. He is holding 3 red balloons.
Alice has long, straight hair. She is holding 5 green balloons.
Ray has straight hair. He is holding 3 purple balloons.
Janine has long, curly hair. She is holding 5 blue balloons.
Tom has light-colored hair. He is holding 4 yellow balloons.

How many balloons can you count on the page? _____

Many people who do a special job wear a special hat. Find the right hat for each worker. Draw a line from each person's head to the correct hat.

What kind of hat is your favorite? Draw it in the box at the bottom of the page.

Match the animal parts on the left with the animals on the right. Write the correct number on each animal.

Finish the pattern 2 more times. Use a pencil to fill in the empty boxes.

X	O	X	O	X	O	O					

Use your crayons to color in the first 6 boxes. Finish the color pattern 2 more times.

red	blue	red	blue	yellow	green			
blue		green			red		yellow	

You can finish this pattern by drawing either a smiling or a frowning face. Complete the pattern 4 more times.

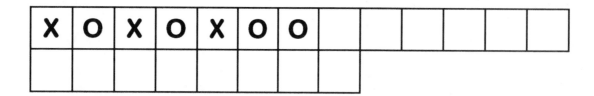

Now you can make up a pattern of your own! Ask a friend to complete the pattern.

Look at the pictures of circles. Each group has a center circle with 6 circles around it. Which center circle is bigger? The one on the left, or the one on the right? You decide.

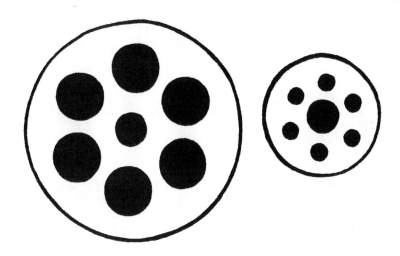

Look at circle A. Look at circle B. Is one bigger than the other? You decide.

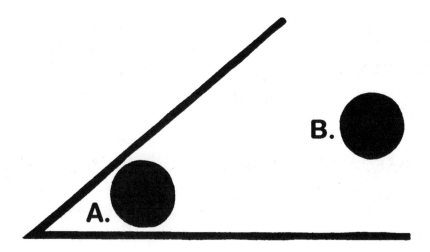

Look at the picture. Look at it again and again. What do you see? Do you see a vase? Do you see something else?

You can show this picture to some of your friends. What does each friend see?

Look at **both** drawings at the same time. Gray spots will appear wherever the lines cross. Now look closely at only the top picture in a place where the lines cross. Is a gray spot still there? What has happened to the spots?

Now look closely at the bottom picture. Are the gray spots still there?

Look at picture number 4. What do you think happened before Don and Randy got into the pool? What might happen when the boys get out of the pool?

You can decide how the story will go from beginning to end. Put a number in the empty square in each of the other pictures. Choose a number from 1 to 3 or 5 to 7. Number 1 will be what you think happened first. Number 7 will be what you think happened last.

You are a good storyteller!

Look at picture number 1. Melissa has just woken up. You can decide how the rest of the story will go after Melissa jumps out of bed.

Put a number in the empty square in each of the other pictures. Choose a number from 2 to 7. Number 2 will be what you think happens next. Number 7 will be what you think happens last.

Your stories are getting better and better!

Julie and Jason are outdoors, playing in the snow. The end of the story is shown in picture number 6. You can decide how the beginning and the middle of the story will go. Number the pictures from 1 to 5 by filling in the empty squares.

Keep telling stories. You are good at it!

To make a peanut butter and jelly sandwich, you would need:

- **two slices of bread**
  - **peanut butter**
    - **jelly**
    - **a table knife**
    - **a plate**

Think about how you would make the sandwich, then look at the pictures below. They are all mixed up. Two pictures do not belong at all! Number the correct pictures in order from 1 to 4. Circle the pictures that don't belong.

Look at the honeycomb maze. Please help the bee get to the honey. There is more than one way for the bee to go. Which is the **shortest** path to the honey?

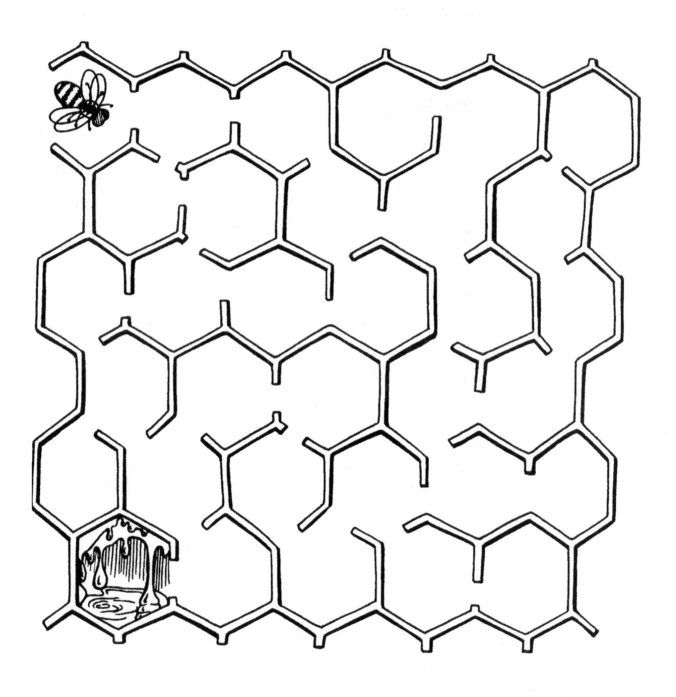

Jack wanted to sell his cow for beans. Toby said he would give Jack 3 bags of beans for his cow. Each of Toby's bags had 5 beans in it. Connie said she would give Jack 2 bags of beans for his cow. Each of her bags had 10 beans in it.

Should Jack sell his cow to Toby or to Connie? Draw a circle around the person you would choose.

How many beans would Jack have if he sold his cow to Toby? _____

How many beans would Jack have if he sold his cow to Connie? _____

Sheena's mother gave her a small box of cookies. There are 12 cookies in the box. Sheena wants to share them with her friends Bobby and Janine. Each child should get the same number of cookies.

Write the number of cookies each child will get on the line near each picture.

Jimmy climbed up to his tree house to read a book and eat his lunch. But all of a sudden the ladder broke!

Look at the pictures below. What should Jimmy do? You can decide. Put a check mark ✔ in each picture that will help Jimmy get down from the tree house.

Did you help Jimmy? Is he happy or sad? Draw a picture in the empty box to show how Jimmy feels.

Suppose you have only 1 candy bar, but there are 8 people who want a piece, including yourself. How many ways could you cut the candy bar into 8 pieces, all the same size? Draw them in the boxes below. Two ways have been done for you.

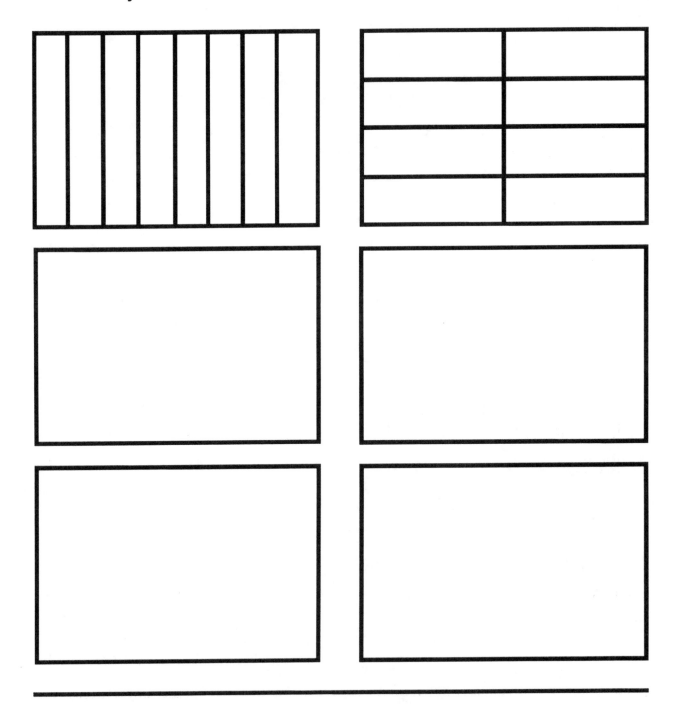

Look at the shapes. See how much money each shape is worth.

A circle ◯ = 5 cents

A rectangle ▭ = 10 cents

A square ☐ = 15 cents

A triangle △ = 25 cents

In the space below, draw a picture that is worth 75 cents.

On another piece of paper, you can draw more pictures. Ask a friend to guess how much each one is worth.

How much is this picture worth? _____

Can you match the **outsides** with the **insides**? Draw a line from each outside picture on the left to its inside picture on the right. One picture is missing. You can draw your own picture in the box.

Can you match the **outsides** with the **insides**? Draw a line from each outside picture on the left to its inside picture on the right.

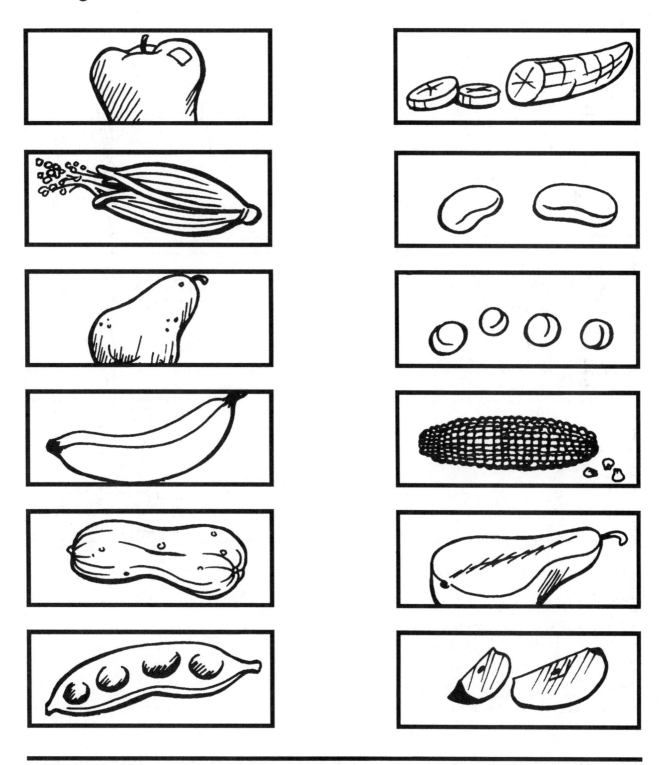

Look at the Family Food Graph. It has 7 parts. You can name the last 2 parts.

Ask the members of your family which **2** foods they like best to eat. Color in 2 different squares for each person in your family. Remember to color in 2 squares for yourself! Use a different color for each food. This will show you which food choices have more filled squares.

Family Food Graph

vegetables											
fruits											
hot dogs											
pizza											
cookies											
_____											
_____											

Which food was chosen the most? _____

Which food was chosen the least? _____

Here are some shapes, but they are not whole. You can find the missing pieces in the box at the bottom of the page. Use your pencil to complete the shapes.

Some pieces can be used to complete more than one shape. Do you know which ones?

How are all the shapes with straight lines alike?

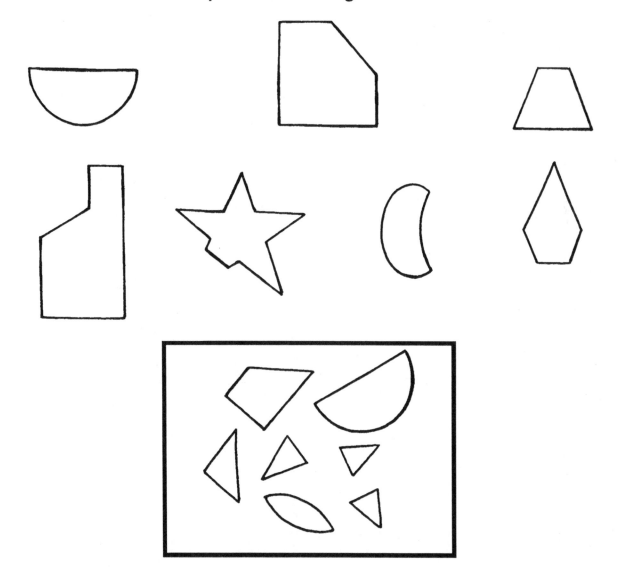

Sometimes the moon is full and whole. It looks like this: ◯. Sometimes we see only part of the moon. It might look like this: ◗. Look at the six moons below with missing parts. Some of the shapes are silly! Draw a circle around the correct missing shape below each moon. Be careful! There might be more than one answer.

Here are some pictures with missing parts. You can find the pieces in the Missing Parts Yard. Draw each missing part in the correct place to complete the pictures.

Look at the animals below. Where would each animal **most** like to be? In the sky, on the ground, or in the water?

Put an **S** on each animal that would be in the sky. Put a **G** on each animal that would be on the ground. Put a **W** on each animal that would be in the water. Be careful—some animals can be in more than one place!

Look at the workers below. Where would be the **best** place for each person to work? In the sky, on the ground, or in the water?

Put an **S** on each worker that would be in the sky. Put a **G** on each worker that would be on the ground. Put a **W** on each worker that would be in the water. Be careful—some workers could be in more than one place!

Beside each picture are the words **hands** and **feet**. Draw a circle around the word that goes with each picture. For some pictures, you might want to choose both words!

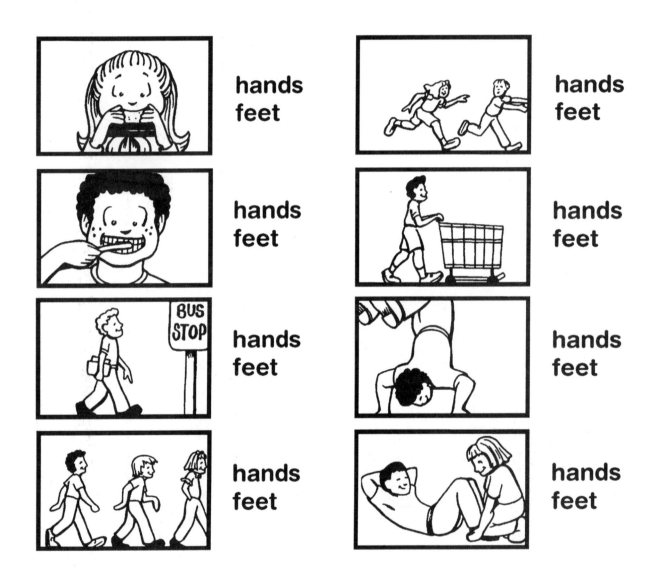

hands
feet

hands
feet

hands
feet

hands
feet

hands
feet

hands
feet

hands
feet

hands
feet

Which would you use, **hands** or **feet**? Look at the pictures below. Draw a circle around each word you choose. For some pictures, you might want to choose both words!

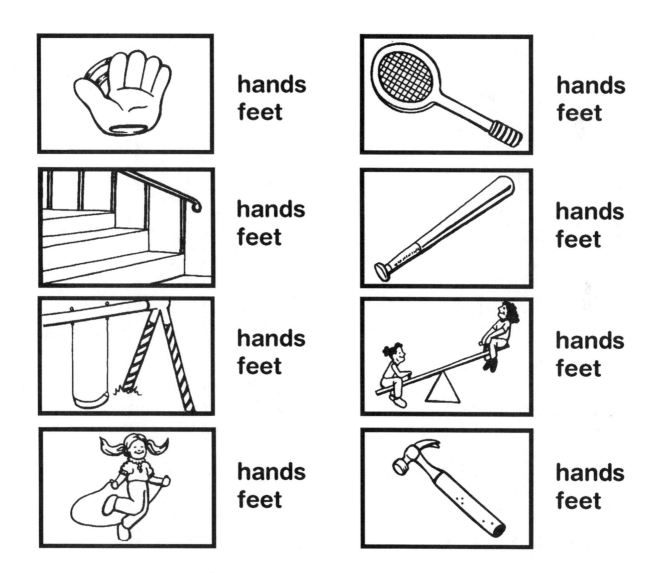

**hands
feet**

**hands
feet**

**hands
feet**

**hands
feet**

**hands
feet**

**hands
feet**

**hands
feet**

**hands
feet**

Look at the pictures. Are the people **working** or **playing**?
You decide. Draw a circle around the word you choose.

working
playing

working
playing

working
playing

working
playing

working
playing

working
playing

Look at the holiday pictures below. Take lots of time. When you are ready, turn the page and look at the same pictures there. Some parts are missing. Circle the missing parts. You can color the pictures.

What holiday is being celebrated? _____

It is Grandpa's birthday. Who is bringing in the cake? Look closely at the silly picture. Draw a circle around all the things that don't make sense. You can color the picture.

Look at the picture. A lot of silly things are going on! Draw a circle around all the things that **do** make sense.

Look at the pictures of flags. How is one different from another? If you would like to, you can make a flag for your family. Draw your family flag in the large space below. Will it have stars or stripes? Will it have animals or people? You can decide. Color your flag and give it a name.

Write the name of your family flag here: _____ .

Here are some pictures from different stories. They are all jumbled up.

One story is "Little Red Riding Hood." Mark all of its pictures with an **L**. Another story is "The Gingerbread Man." Mark all of its pictures with a **G**. The third story is "The Three Bears." Mark all of its pictures with a **B**.

You can color the pictures. What colors will you use?

Look at the story pictures again. Tell yourself the stories as you look at them. Write **1**, **2**, or **3** under each picture to show the correct order.

_____   _____   _____

_____   _____   _____

_____   _____   _____

Look at the groups of pictures. You can put them in order. Write **1**, **2**, or **3** under each picture. They could be in more than one order. Choose the way that you like best.

Look at the pictures below. See if you can find a match for each picture, from one row to the other. Draw a line from the picture on the left to its matching picture on the right.

The children are going to put on a Halloween play. They need to make costumes. They want to put up decorations and make invitations. They want to serve snacks, too.

Look at the picture. You decide what the children will need for their play. Circle those parts of the picture.

Look at all the letters of the alphabet. Each letter has a number below it. It is a code. If you solve the code, you will find the words to a song. On the lines below, write the correct letter that goes with each number.

A	B	C	D	E	F	G	H	I	J
1	3	5	7	9	11	13	15	17	19

K	L	M	N	O	P	Q	R	S	T
21	23	2	4	6	8	10	12	14	16

U	V	W	X	Y	Z
18	20	22	24	25	26

___ ___ , ___ ___ ___ ___ ___ , ___ ___ ,
 6   15   22 15 9 12 9   6   15

___ ___ ___ ___ ___ ___ ___ ___ ___ ___
22 15 9 12 9   15 1 14   2 25

___ ___ ___ ___ ___ ___ ___ ___ ___
23 17 16 16 23 9   7 6 13

___ ___ ___ ___ ?
13 6 4 9

Have you solved the code?
Can you sing the rest of the song?

Look at the big box filled with letters. If you look closer, you will see words hiding there. Look at the word box below it to help you find the hidden words. Draw a ring around each word you find. The first one is done for you.

M	A	P	S	K	I	D
Y	E	T	L	N	X	E
D	E	N	I	C	A	N
P	I	G	D	F	O	R
R	I	P	W	I	G	A
A	S	A	I	D	Y	T
T	E	N	E	T	H	E
I	T	D	S	L	I	D

yet map skid can wig
ten net it slid den
rip as the for pig

Can you find any other words? What new words can you see when you read the puzzle from top to bottom?

Look at the animal pictures. Write the correct animal name under each one. Where do these animals live?

How many different words could you make from each name? Write the words on the lines below them.

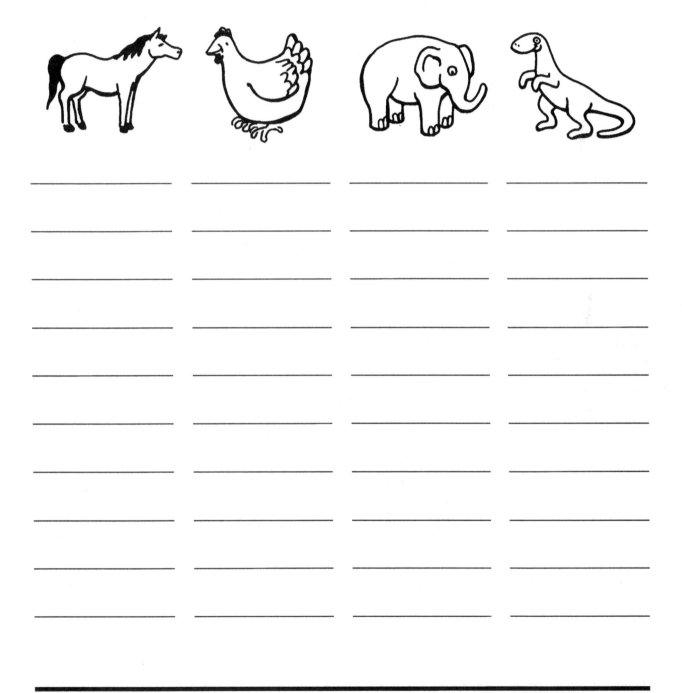

Here are some definitions. A definition explains what a word means. Below each definition are 3 words with matching pictures. Circle the word that goes **best** with each definition. Write it on the line.

A) A part of a blouse or a shirt that goes around the neck.

_____

cuff 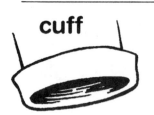   **hem**    **collar**

B) A wild animal that has hooves.

_____

deer    **bear**    **lion**

C) A sound made when someone is happy or sees something funny.

_____

scream    **smile**    **laugh**

Can you complete the alphabet sentences below? Look at the letters A and B that have been done for you. Finish the others by filling in the lines. Use words that go with the letters. On another piece of paper, draw pictures of your own for each alphabet letter.

A is for Anna because she is an angry ant.
B is for ball because it is big and bouncy.

C is for _____ because _____ .

D is for _____ because _____ .

E is for _____ because _____ .

F is for _____ because _____ .

G is for _____ because _____ .

H is for _____ because _____ .

Use another sheet of paper and go all the way to Z!

Look at the funny pictures below. Now look at the word box. Each word has a number beside it. Match each word and number with a picture. Put the correct number on the line below each picture.

footstool 1   fishbowl 2   butterfly 3
eardrum 4   catfish 5   horsefly 6   hatbox 7

Look at the pictures of the bear, summertime, the blanket, and the pot of warm soup. Now look at the word box. Write the words that belong with each picture on the lines below it.

_____   _____   _____   _____

_____   _____   _____   _____

_____   _____   _____   _____

_____   _____   _____   _____

swim   bowl   furry   carrots   bed
picnics   soft   paws   growl   shorts   spoon
wild   night   sleep   chicken   sandals

Jane and her friends are dressed up for Halloween. Look at their pictures on this page and the next. The children's names all begin with the letter **J**. Read the clues, then write each child's name on the line below his or her picture. Please color their costumes.

Jane and Jenny are clowns. Their costumes are different colors.

Jamal is a pumpkin. He has a brown stalk on his head.

John is a mail carrier. Where is his blue mailbag? Please draw one.

Joshua is a pirate. Part of his costume is missing. Please finish it.

——————   ——————   ——————   ——————   ——————

Judy, Jill, and Jan are witches. Judy has a pointed hat.
Jill has shoes with turned-up toes. Be careful! Which witch
is which?
Joe and Jacob are ghosts. Jacob is wearing boots.

————— ————— ————— ————— —————

Here is an **across** puzzle. Look at the clues. Fill in the correct words in the boxes going across. Look for the **down** words near the clues. They can help you solve the puzzle.

Across

1. Spiders spin a _____ .

3. Spiders have eight _____ .

5. Spiders don't walk, they _____ .

Down

big

saw

lock

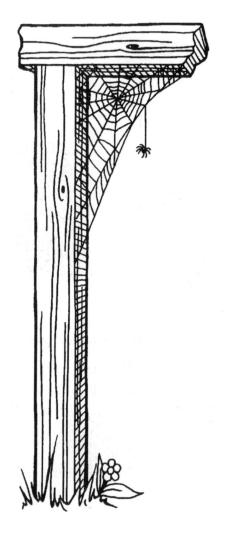

Here is an **across** puzzle. Look at the clues. Fill in the correct words in the boxes going across. Look for the **down** words near the clues. They can help you solve the puzzle.

Across	Down
1. A small horse.	ate
4. A horse's walk.	was
6. Not old.	note
8. Horse food.	only

Here is an **across** puzzle. Look at the clues. Fill in the correct words in the boxes going across. Look for the **down** words near the clues. They can help you solve the puzzle.

Across   Down

1. Ducks like to _____ .   rake

2. Ducks are often seen in _____ .   that

5. Ducks say, " _____ ."   sew

Look at the two rows of shapes. Try to find the matching pairs. Draw a line from each shape on the left to the same shape on the right.

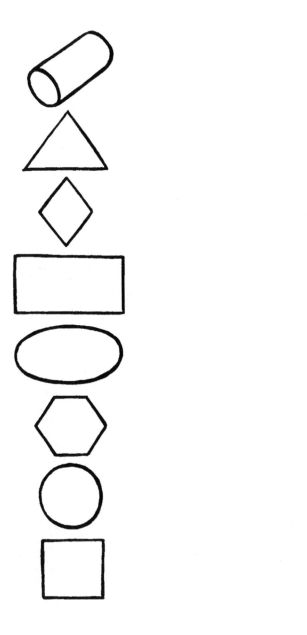

Look at the groups of snowflakes below. Which of the small snowflakes matches the big snowflake above it? Draw a circle around each small snowflake that is a match.

Look at the first group of birds resting on the telephone wire. Color each of the birds.

Below, find the group of birds that matches the one you colored. Draw a ring around it.

Look at the chair pattern. Each chair has 4 legs. When someone is sitting on a chair, how many legs can you see? In each empty box, write the number of legs that you would see if the pattern was finished 2 more times. How many legs would there be in the whole row if each box was filled in? _____

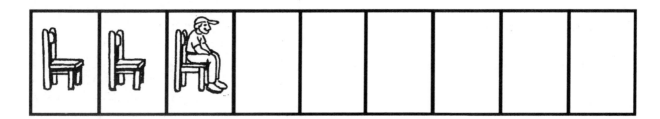

Make a color pattern using all the circles. You can decide how to color them in. Make your color pattern 3 times.

Look at the fruit pattern. Draw the fruits to continue the pattern once more. Color the pieces of fruit. Keep going to the last square.

Read the words from favorite stories on the left side of this page. Look at the pictures on the right. Match each group of words with a picture. Draw a line between them.

WHO SAID THAT?

I SAID THAT!

"Slow and steady wins the race."

"My, Grandmother, what big eyes you have!"

"Fee, fi, fo, fum!"

"He preferred to smell the flowers."

"And someone's eaten my porridge all up!"

"My, what a good boy am I!"

Read the words from favorite stories on the left side of this page. Look at the pictures on the right. Match each group of words with a picture. Draw a line between them.

WHO SAID THAT?

I SAID THAT!

"His mother put him to bed and gave him some chamomile tea."

"I'll huff, and I'll puff . . ."

"Who's that trip-trapping over my bridge?"

"Mirror, mirror, on the wall, who's the fairest one of all?"

"Run, run, as fast as you can . . ."

Page 5:

deer	cow	dog
cat	bike	baby
mouse	bunny	fox
skunk	tree	wagon

Page 6:
red = bad, Tad, sad, mad, Dad, had
blue = bed, Ned, led, red
yellow = Sam, yam, Pam, ham
green = mat, bat

Page 7:
flag, fish, milk, feet, toes, frog, pan

Page 8:
Little Boy Blue, come blow your horn, the Sheep's in the meadow, the cow's in the corn.
The kitten was born in the tall corn. Sally gave the kitten her worn, torn blanket.
or Sally gave the kitten her torn, worn blanket.

Page 9:

Page 10:

Page 11:

Page 12:

Page 13:

Pages 14-15:
1 = cow, chicken, sheep, pig
2 = owl, deer, fox, raccoon
3 = elephant, pony, lion

Page 16:
Allison is one of the 10 children in her class. She didn't send a card to herself!

Page 17:
Dad's chain is the longest. Andy's chain is the shortest. There are 6 paper chains in all. Jim has 14 circles in his chain. Andy has 3 circles in his chain.

Page 18:
Purple is the longest bar. It has 8 colored squares.

Page 19:
There are 20 balloons in all.

Ray   Alice   Bonnie   Tom   Janine

Page 20:

Page 21:

Page 22:

red	blue	red	blue	yellow	green	red	blue	red
blue	yellow	green	red	blue	red	blue	yellow	green

Page 23:
This is an optical illusion, which means your eyes are playing a trick on you. Both circles are the same size. They look different because of the sizes of the circles around them. In the second puzzle, circles A. and B. are the same size.

Page 24:
This is an optical illusion. When you look at the white part, you see the vase. When you look at the dark part, you probably see two people.

Page 25:
This is an optical illusion. The gray spots only appear in the top picture when you force your eyes to look at both pictures at once. When you look at only the bottom picture, the gray spots always appear to be there.

Pages 26-28:
Answers will vary.

Page 29:

Page 30:

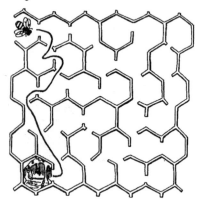

Page 31:
Jack would have 15 beans if he sold his cow to Toby. Jack would have 20 beans if he sold his cow to Connie.

Page 32:
Each child gets 4 cookies.

Page 33:
Answers will vary.

Page 34:
Answers will vary. Here are some of the ways the candy bar could be cut.

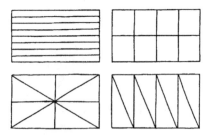

Page 35:
The picture is worth 95 cents.

Page 36:

Page 37:

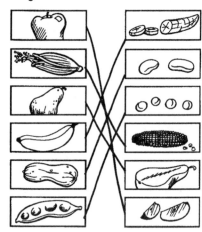

Page 38:
Answers will vary.

Page 39:

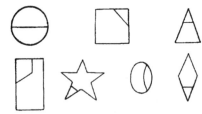

The triangle, the star, and the diamond each have pieces that are the same.
All the shapes with straight lines have corners, or angles.

Page 40:

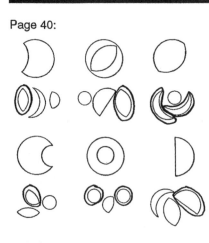

Page 41:

Page 42:
Answers will vary.

Page 43:
Answers will vary.

Page 44:

Page 45:

Page 46:
Answers will vary.

Page 48:

What holiday is being celebrated?
The 4th of July.

Page 49:

Page 50:

Page 51:
Answers will vary.

Page 52:

Page 53:

Page 54:
Answers will vary.

Page 55:

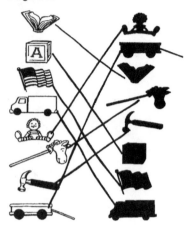

Page 56:
Answers will vary.

Page 57:
OH, WHERE, OH, WHERE HAS MY
LITTLE DOG GONE?

Page 58:
The new words from top to bottom
are: RAT, AT, IS, SET, PAN, AND,
LID, HI, TED, ED.

Page 59:
The horse and chicken live on a farm.
The elephant lives in the jungle. The
dinosaur is not alive anymore. There
are many possible words. Here are a
few.
horse: hose, rose, so, hoe
chicken: chick, hen, check, neck
elephant: leap, ant, pant, pet
dinosaur: sour, our, in, run

Page 60:
A) collar
B) deer
C) laugh

Page 61:
Answers will vary.

Page 62:

Page 63:

growl	swim	bed	carrots
paws	picnics	night	bowl
wild	shorts	sleep	spoon
furry	sandals	soft	chicken

Page 64:

John   Jamal   Jane or Jenny   Jenny or Jane   Joshua

Page 65:

Jill   Jacob   Joe   Judy   Jan

Page 66:

w	e	b	
		i	
l	e	g	s
o		a	
c	r	a	w	l
k			

Page 67:

	p	o	n	y
a		o		
t	r	o	t	
e		n	e	w
		l		a
h	a	y		s

Page 68:

s	w	i	m
e			
w	a	t	e	r
		h		a
q	u	a	c	k
		t		e

Page 69:

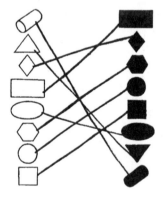

Page 70:

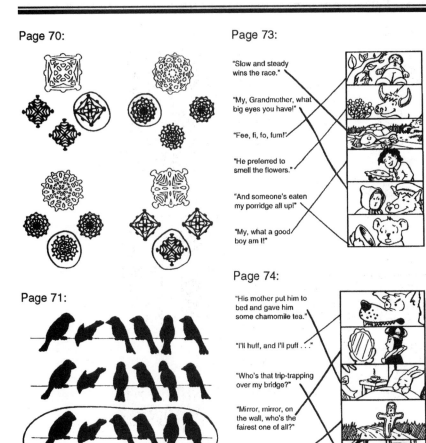

Page 73:

"Slow and steady wins the race."

"My, Grandmother, what big eyes you have!"

"Fee, fi, fo, fum!"

"He preferred to smell the flowers."

"And someone's eaten my porridge all up!"

"My, what a good boy am I!"

Page 74:

"His mother put him to bed and gave him some chamomile tea."

"I'll huff, and I'll puff . . ."

"Who's that trip-trapping over my bridge?"

"Mirror, mirror, on the wall, who's the fairest one of all?"

"Run, run, as fast as you can . . ."

Page 71:

Page 72:
In the first pattern, there would be 42 legs in the row.

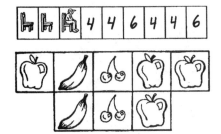